Light & Shade

Light & Shade

J. H. B. PEEL

ROBERT HALE · LONDON

© *J. H. B. Peel 1976*

First published in Great Britain 1976

ISBN 0 7091 5826 2

Robert Hale & Company
Clerkenwell House
45/47 Clerkenwell Green
London EC1 0HT

Printed in Great Britain by Bristol Typesetting Co. Ltd,
Barton Manor, St. Philips, Bristol

CONTENTS

HARVEST

In spring my heart went forth to plough,
And here the grain is hoarded;
It does not greatly matter now
What merits are awarded.

My song, the rod and staff of life,
With vigour still sustains me;
Acclaim has ceased to be my strife;
Silence no longer pains me.

Should two or three partake of these
That were my lifetime reaping,
I shall receive their courtesies
In ever-kindly keeping.

And yet so proud my song has grown
Upon such humble living,
That truly to itself alone
Belongs this harvest-giving.

DAMOCLES

How slim the cord
That holds the sword;
How deep the dread
Above the head.
The blade will fall
At beck-and-call
Of random intervention
That kills without intention.

We seldom raise
Our eyes, nor gaze
Too closely, lest
We grow distressed;
Instead, we stir
A blind ember,
Warming the predicament
Of our human tenement.

Poor Tom's a-cold,
And Lear old,
And Gloucester blind,
And all mankind
Out on the heath
Naked beneath
Whatever lurks above them,
And does not seem to love them.

THE MASTER MASON

Before the breeding of the Bomb,
In years when God was still enthroned
Among the hearts of Christendom,
Men built an abbey, steep and stoned;
And one of many masons there
(For whom his craft was very life)
Longed, with a humble pride, to share
Some part in beauty rising rife
Through chancel, chapel, buttress, nave,
Clerestory, rood screen, and the tower
Whose peak surged upward like a wave
Of unpremeditated power.

But not for him the great desire,
A place where all might see his art;
The man, though worthy of his hire,
Was sent to labour far apart
From them that carved the timber roof,
Or wrought the turret stonely-lipped.
His portion was to work aloof,
Deep in an unfrequented crypt
Where, should they come at all, his kind
Would scarcely see the thing he made
By one dim window partly blind,
And in the darkness half-afraid.

The lonely mason soon rebelled
Against his unregarded plight;
While others in the sun excelled,
He wilted in a nether-night.

Then from the darkness came a voice,
Pitched between sorrow and a smile:
"My son, take courage, and rejoice,
For I perceive the hidden style.
And if indeed to me is made
The gift which I bestowed on you,
What matter where it be displayed,
For I am everywhere in view?"

The marvelling mason heard, and stood
Rebuked by shame, yet raised by love;
Was he not of the brotherhood
Who worked in sunlight high above?

From that day forth he plied his skill
With fervour which the years arrayed
As reapers on a window-sill
And corn-sheaves in a colonnade
So carved that each appeared to sing
For joy, that art should so release
—Out of a dumb and darkened thing—
Patterns of beauty, power, and peace.

Nor did his harvest end with death,
For Time untopped the abbey towers,
And on the rubble underneath
Scattered the dust of many flowers
But not his own, for in that place
Where once he laboured far from sight,
Men met his corn-sheaves face-to-face,
And were astounded by the light

Of such unconquerable love
Imprisoned as it were a dove
In barred and blinded darkness, yet
Serving the hidden Olivet
From whence it came and for whose sake
If shone there still, that all might take
Comfort and courage.

                       Master mason,
Hear now in heaven our orison:
Thy lamp is lit; thy work is well;
And we that still in darkness dwell
Are thankful for the lesson taught,
Which served within its sphere, and wrought
Humbly with pride, and did not yield
Until the stooks bestrode the field.

WINTER SUNSHINE

The sun,
Whose race indeed seemed run,
Now casts a golden-spun
Glow on the fallow dun.

Young wheat,
Well-disciplined in neat
Crocodile, leaps to greet
An unaccustomed heat.

Bare trees
Create a besom frieze;
Puddles are blue-eyed seas;
Cows sunbathe on their knees.

Rare days
That shine like this, win praise
From countrymen whose ways
Follow a muddy haze.

CASKET

When the summer leaves are low
In an unremembered snow;
When youth's citadel has gone,
And the dreams of Avalon;
Then amid the rubble gazing
At a ruin so amazing,
Men may find this threnody,
And wonder idly: " Who was she?"
So your beauty shall abide
Safe awhile from time and tide
In this casket, which I make
For those wondering men to take.

CONDEMNED TO LIFE

Regard the sick of soul
Whose unapparent sore
Conceals a strident mole
Uncivilly at war.

With infinite noblesse
Oblige them manyfold
Whose epic of distress
Is patiently untold.

They would not, yet they must;
A worm has sapped the rose;
Release their hidden trust
Whom only thorns enclose.

SAILOR'S WIFE

Over the water clearly
I heard a woman singing
Low to her infant, cheerly
The gay world's comfort bringing.

Alone she plied her dinghy
Across the harbour lithely,
Through wavelets lawn-like springy
That cradled the man-child blithely:

He in a basket, beyond
The sea spray, pleasure-cruising;
In all the world the second
Mariner of her choosing.

RETURN TICKET

Teach me, that I may learn to die,
Not with an intellectual eye,
But utterly in every part
Of so-called body, mind, and heart.

Teach me to feel my folded hands
Within the wooden box that stands
Over a fire that shall consume
The corpse's customary doom.

Teach me to wean myself away
From what I love: the work, the play,
The sea, the hills, the song, the friend;
Teach me that all beginnings end.

Teach me to know that all things are
A brief and meteoric star
Seen for an instant on the skies
Before its evanescence dies.

Then, having taught so, let me learn
The skills with which dead men return
And once again accept the strife
Of never-everlasting life.

BIRD OF DAWNING

Upon a morning once in May,
Glancing up for'ard,
I saw a clipper in the bay
Nor'west-by-nor'ard.

No sound she made, that dawning bird;
No engine ranting;
Her song was sung without a word,
Silently canting.

The beauty of her bow alone
Carving each white horse
Like whetted razor on a hone,
Called back the old Norse.

We have no vessel now to match
That tall-rigged glory,
Nor any yarn of any watch
Capping her story.

INDUSTRIAL REVOLUTION

Back-to-back and face-to-face
These mean houses sourly trace
Our rugged Island Story,
Its grandeur and its glory,
The coal-and-cotton reapers,
The nation of shopkeepers.

Here through fourteen hours a day
Jack and Jill drudged life away;
At four years old, their children
Joined the gaunt gang, to leaven
The bread and precious penny
Wrung from a spinning jenny.

Hopeless, hungry, stunted, cowed,
Clogged and shawled beneath a shroud
Of smoke and stench and grimey
Milltown façades and slimey
Waterway-walks, they wilted
Listlessly sad and silted.

Yet their loving-kindness stood
Firm as virtue's hardihood;
Vice and despair and squalor
Did not suppress the valour
Of that grim band of brothers
Who helped themselves and others.

Such the power and such the wealth;
Such the beauty and the health;
Such the prosperous attar
Rising from Mammon's altar,
The incense of an epoch
That sacrificed to Moloch.

MIRAGE

I could have sworn that it was snow,
So white the river seemed
With icicles arrayed to glow
Like blades of glass that gleamed.
But I was wrong, and she was right
... The Moon, that from her prime
Descanted on the summer night
Inaudibly, with rime.

QUANTUM THEORY

I am assessing you
With analytic eye
That sifts the chiefly true
From what was largely lie.

First, I compute your age,
For arteries conspire
To regulate the rage
Of striving and desire.

The timbre of your speech
Suggests a place of birth,
And whether you will reach
The richer rungs on earth.

The rhythm of your walk,
The murmur of your hands,
Reveal a tone of talk
Among genetic glands.

When the deep traits are clear,
I diagnose a course,
Gauging your skill to steer
The temperamental horse.

Yet all the atoms have
Their quanta as they fall,
And you may re-behave
Like Saul when he was Paul.

So, while you turn on me
Your own incisive gaze,
Allow that men may be
More than the sum of traits.

APRIL

The land's alive again,
Though gently.
A blackbird down the lane,
Intently
Stirring the newborn leaves,
Aslant
Their filtered sunlight weaves
A chant
Invisibly. The tang
Of March
—As though the blackbird sang
To parch
The rime of wintry death—
Retreats.
A new lamb finds its breath,
And bleats.

BENEATH THE SKIN

Man's gay veneer
Is very thin;
He throbs with fear
Beneath the skin.

He fears to lose
His youthful ways,
The smile that woos,
The charm that sways.

He fears old age,
The sad descent,
The finished page,
The passion spent.

He fears disease,
The swift (or slow)
Stroke that decrees
His overthrow.

Fearing to fear,
He craves release
In death's austere
And lifeless peace.

Pity us all;
Our lives are led
Under the thrall
Of hidden dread.

SONG AND DANCE

These
Tall beech trees
Serenely at their ease
Are welcoming the April breeze
With limbs outstretched in cordial courtesies.

Green
Leaves now lean
Windward, and then careen,
And then sway back again, their sheen
Showing the vein-like twigs that shine between.

Spring
Hears them sing
Like birds whose whispering wing,
Though always restless, does not wring
A protest from the roots' deep anchoring.

Chance
Winds advance
To join with song, and prance
In spritely yet becoming stance,
Till Dunsinane and Birnam seem to dance.

STONEHENGE

They built no wall to shield them from the wind,
Nor raised a roof against the sun and rain;
The centuries were powerless to rescind
This relic of religion on the Plain.
From western Wales (men say) the rock was hewn,
Then hauled, then shipped on rafts across the sea.
What piety and fortitude were strewn
Along the path of such gaunt symmetry?
What keen-eyed superstition poised the stone
To balance on the rising of the sun?
By what dim myth were deities made known?
What sacerdotal sacrifice was done?
Here Tintern and here Charterhouse are seen
Prefigured in a tower that does not lean.

EQUATION

I would not have you less,
I would not have you more,
Since in your equalness
I find the perfect flaw
. . . That, being flesh and bone,
You are the same as I
Whose heart will mime a stone
Till laughter mocks the lie.
So, imperfection makes
Perfectibility
Which from my favour takes
Itself bestowed on me.

THE BRITISH ISLES

As in a vision, I beheld
The British Islands, set
County by county, clearly spelled
In beauty's alphabet.

At John o'Groat's I saw the wide
Acres of farm and firth
Wherein for days a man might stride
Alone upon the Earth.

I saw the loch along the glen,
I smelled the heather-swale,
I heard the skirling pipes of men
Descended from the Gael.

Out of a troubled sea the blue
Mountains of Mourne arose,
Where warlike poets sought a rue
For wounds that would not close.

I saw the peel towers of the north,
A no-man's land for men
Who, when the raiders ventured forth,
Struck with the strength of ten.

Westward through snow the pinnacles
Of Lakeland rose to pray
Imponderable canticles
Without a word to say.

I saw the English backbone, each
Vertebra in the sun
. . . The Pennine Range, half-out-of-reach
So high its race was run.

All over Wales I looked, and heard
The mountains and the mines
Singing their legends undeterred
By Time's corrosive tines.

I saw the Marches, fierce and fey,
Where Cymru and the Sais
Came down of old that they might slay,
Or be a sacrifice.

In Lincolnshire I saw the folds
And shepherds with their crook,
Where Tennyson had sung the Wolds
As blithely as a brook.

Peakland I saw, the Wonders there,
From ramparts high above
Old Izaak Walton's spinning lair
Beside the gentle Dove.

I saw the coloured counties lie
Like jewels beneath the sun
. . . Wrekin and Mynd and stripling Wye
And Severn silver-spun.

Mellow in moonlight, warm by day,
The Cotswold hamlets stood
Like hospices along the way
To beauty's brotherhood.

I saw pink-coated foxy folk
Hunting the midmost Shires
Through falling leaves and rising smoke
And miles of squires and spires.

Norfolk and Suffolk prospered still,
A fertile plot of earth,
Where Constable embalmed a mill,
And Nelson came to birth.

I looked toward the Kentish coast
That harboured Celts and Huns
And many another savage host
Whereof we are the sons.

How beautiful old Wessex lay,
Poised between grass and heath;
White clouds above a shingle bay;
The English Moat beneath.

And last, from Cornwall, came a view
That climbed as high as heaven
. . . Saint Mawes, Saint Anthony, Saint Ewe,
Saint Agnes, and Saint Levan.

Is there an island on this star
So small and yet so fair?
Can beauty beckon near and far
With finer sights to share?

Such is Britain, a national trust
In which we are partakers;
Shall Mammon set the moth to rust
Among those pleasant acres?

ANNO DOMINI

He knew that he was growing old at last,
Because he knew that he was growing young;
Down the deep chimney of a distant past
Came Father Christmas, with a gift-sack slung
Over his scarlet shoulder. Then were heard
The wise men and the shepherds and the high
Tenor of Gabriel uttering the Word,
And many voices singing in the sky.
Dreaming, he shared the first of all Noels,
And with the faithful rose and came again
To Bethlehem amid the sound of bells
Pealing a joyful and triumphant strain.
Then through the stable door he glimpsed a light,
And in the manger-cradle saw a child,
And all the wonderland was wearing white,
And nothing was defeated nor defiled.
Thus toward second childhood he advanced
While firelight flickered, and the snowflakes danced.

SUMMER RAIN

At last the long-awaited rain comes down,
Slaking a soil with weeds for crown
Drought-high; yet this grey frown
Will never drown
The brown

Pastures and ponds and fissured lawns that hiss
Contentedly while raindrops kiss
Each root least any miss
The boon of this
Remiss

And fickle-flowing fountain whose noblesse
Succours the seasonal distress
With chivalrous caress
As though to stress
Largesse.

MYSTIQUE

A snowflake stooped to bring it
... The echo of a song
From birds that would not sing it
While winter nights were long.

But when I heard the omen
Of that imagined grace,
Earth was afire with numen
From an unearthly place.

Aloud within the silence
Of pain's ubiquity,
Joy, with a rapt impatience,
Saw what it could not see.

It was an In Extremis
Transfigured to recite
The mystical Excelsis
Of infinite delight.

NEW YEAR'S DAY

Under the earth great things are happening;
There the daffodils sit, sharpening
Swords that, having pierced the soil,
Are trumpets of the spring. There toil
The bluebells at their muted ringing,
And snowdrops like a blizzard, springing
Upward, not down, slower than snow
To melt away. There—while a low
Scowl-sky threatens frost—there smile
Crocus and primrose that, with file
More fragile than the earth, erupt
Little volcanoes; there the cupped
Acorns are mountain-making mice,
And every celandine a dice
Shaking to show a six in spring.
Though men are deaf, earth's anvils ring.

SIMILE

I love you, as a man desires the moon
Although he knows he cannot reach so far;
I love you, as a man desires the noon
While still he walks the night without a star.

I love you, as a man when he would take
A gossamer of delicate display;
I love you, as a man when he would break
Whatever mountain barred his lawful way.

I love you, as a man who has not worn
His heart upon a sleeve he lightly gives;
I love you, as a man who has been born
To cherish what he treasures while he lives.

I love you, as a man in whom the dove
Lay down beside a lion within his lair;
I love you, as a man was meant to love
The woman who is fallible and fair.

THE LAMP

If any man, woman, or child
Is roaming homeless through this wild
Night of antagonistic snow,
And if they happen to see the glow
From the hurricane lamp beside my door
(I always light it, just before
Dusk), then let them cease to roam,

And make for that lamp as they would for a home
For the homeless who in bitter plight
Crave the fellowship of firelight,
And food, and one who knows what it is
To lack those things on a night like this.

HAUNTED HOUSE

I listen to the rain
Whose rhythm overhead
Recites a cry of pain
That is uncomforted.

The walls and roof are dry,
Windows and door stand fast,
Yet still I hear a cry
Descanting on the past.

Like travellers lost at night,
The very tears of things
Hammer this wuthered heigh'
With wild importunings.

No tower was built so well,
Nor massive armoury,
That either could repel
Besieging memory.

LANDFALL

From skies as blue as Avalon
The clarity of summer shone
With fierce benevolence upon
My tethered ship at anchor
Within a Cornish harbour.

The gulls like piping bo'suns played
A fanfare and a serenade
For every sailor that had made
His landfall in a county
Whose beauty is its bounty.

The ranks of west-wind waves advanced
Like crested stallions that pranced
And by their gay gavotte enhanced
The metronomic motion
Of that pacific ocean.

The clifftop reapers stooked the corn,
The fruit was ripe, the sheep were shorn,
And upward into joy was borne
The ship of gladness surging
Upon an utmost urging.

So many moons ago; and yet
This mariner does not forget
The suns of yesteryear that set
Faint as a scent remembered
Of roses long Decembered.

HAIL AND FAREWELL

Above the hush
Of dumb midwinter, hear
This missel-thrush
Intent to praise the year
And bury it with elegies
Of unrepining harmonies.

Against the storm
His voice is pitched, to keep
Our comfort warm
Within the cold and deep
Darkness of Advent, till the days
Suckle the sun's reviving rays.

No other song
So stirs the season. Earth,
Wrapt in her long
Gestation of rebirth,
Attends the shrill importuning
For safe deliverance of spring.

Ring out, brave sound!
Defy the gale, the snow,
The frozen ground.
Let the loud north wind blow
Your *Ave* to the year now done,
Your *Salve* to an unborn one.

COMPLINE

A quiet conscience sleeps well
On the night's unruly breast,
As it were a sanctus bell
Summoning itself to rest.

Few so supple, they can be
Bounden to the law and yet
Broad of mind and therefore free
From a legal alphabet.

None so saintly but shall stir
At the midnight of their hour,
There to sup with Lucifer
Seeking whom he may devour.

God the Father, God the Son,
God the Holy Spirit be
Symbols of a self at one
With its multiplicity.

RECIPE

Make her so gay, she will perceive
The timeless tragedy of Eve.

Make her so sad, she will rejoice
Hearing the laughter in her voice.

Make her so wise, she will create
Whatever may be made of fate.

Make her so foolish, she will know
Precisely how far not to go.

Make her so trustful, she will dare
To tame the tigress in her lair.

Make her so worldly, she will sense
An atmosphere of innocence.

Make her to love me, there to find
Whatever else she has in mind.

REQUIESCANT

In the land of long repose,
Where the buried people lie,
Not a soul among them knows
What it is to live and die.

Ashen embers in the earth,
All are sheer unconsciousness
As before their parents' birth
All were uncreatedness,

Free from terror and from pain,
Free from guilt and grief and greed
And the stony-grounded grain
And the bandaged wounds that bleed.

Yet the people cannot know
That they dwell in high estate,
Safe forever from the low
Incivility of fate.

AULD AND NEW LANG SYNE

Old friend, at your fire in the smithy among the far fells,
Strike out on the anvil the years as they upwardly fly;
What times we have shared when the summering sheep
                                   rang their bells;
What times when the wintering pinkcoats went cantering
                                   by!

We rode a wide way from the north to the south of this
                                   land;
We followed the Romans; we walked in the tracks of
                                   the Celt;
We watched the stars shine on the estuary's ebb-tiding
                                   sand;
We heard the dumb blizzard that whitened a bracken-
                                   brown veldt.

Up mountains we clambered, and down to the shores of
the lake;
In cottage and manor we sat for a while at our ease;
We gossiped with shepherds alone in a deer-dappled
brake;
We stared in rapt silence while autumn set fire to the trees.

And shall we not hope once again to proceed on our
way,
To visit some eyrie-like church in the heart of the hills,
To watch while a sunset suffuses the last of the day,
To hear while a cuckoo-call romps through the echoing
ghylls?

Strike on, though we both of us long since out-galloped
our prime.
Hammer your anvil, my friend, while I send this reply,
Remembering many a solemn or heigh-ho old time
In the saddle together while larks were aloud on the sky.

OUT IN THE SNOW

Out in the snow by starlight
The crunching rabbits creep
Over a whitewashed meadow
That prints their paws.

Icicles cling to branches
Like stalactites that play
Casual music crisply
With any breeze.

Feet on the farmyard flatten
A moon reflected there
In puddled oceans frozen
From shore to shore.

Embalmed alive, the snowscape
Awaits an Easter Day
Proving the resurrection
Of wintry faith.

ALL OVER ENGLAND

All over England the blackbirds are singing
Songs of a spring-land delightedly ringing
In time with the bluebells whose azure anew spells
Sunlight and laughter and summer thereafter.

All over England the blackbirds are rhyming
With grassland and lingland, their carillon chiming
A music for June days whose lyrical tune plays
Tenor and alto for rivers to echo.

All over England the blackbirds are flying
Loud on a wing-land so rifely supplying
That England all over is covered in clover
Fields where the bee sups on cowslips and kingcups.

PROGRESS REPORT

In many ways the world improves;
On balance, every year reveals
Less suffering and selfishness,
More insight and solicitude.

Cliques may conspire to play the fool,
The anarchist, the murderer;
Tyrants may darken half the earth;
And multitudes may run amok.

Yet, in the quietness of his home,
The common man grows slowly up,
Imperceptibly hour by hour,
Century after century.

If he can curb the ruling class,
The rampant mob, the current creed,
He may prevail, and find himself
Governed by wise self-mastery.

SHAKESPEARE

Not without right you tower above us all
Who in our fashion work with English words;
No other voice can overtake your call,
The eagle and the nightingale of birds,
Peerless and yet not flawless, for you were
As mortal as your own immortal cast,
Those names which through the world's wide
household share
A mint condition that was meant to last.
Excelling all the rest, you have excelled
Your self, as corn out-tops its native acre.
Your self is now by other selves upheld;
Macbeth and Desdemona dwarf their maker;
And William Shakespeare is a sleight-of-signs
Embalmed between his own eternal lines.

BUSINESS AS USUAL

Christ with indignant lash
Scattered the tawdry trash
And itchy-fingered cash
Offered at any price
As Mammon's sacrifice.

Would he might come once more
To raze the market store
That shames the temple door,
Set there by greedy palms
Open for vulgar alms.

But men have learned to bless
Mammon's unrighteousness;
Fawningly they caress
The tentacle that gloats
While it assails their throats.

Money is God supreme,
And Trade its sacred theme;
Mammon has skimmed the cream
From beauty and noblesse
And simple happiness.

LISTEN

Can you hear the grass growing?
Can you hear the flake snowing?
Can you hear the corn springing?
Can you hear the vine clinging?
The setting Sun? The axis Earth?
The thought conceived? The moral worth?
The growth of love? The glance of grief?
The faith? The doubt? The disbelief?
Men have forgotten how to reach
Beyond the barriers of speech.

THE GREEN ROAD

The road goes straight at a rollicking gait
Like a ribbon draped over switchback hills;
Yet it stands sedate
And content to wait
On miles that are grist to its moveless mills.

The grass grows green
In a peaceable scene,
For nobody uses the road, except
As a way between
Two linneys that lean
Where lambs are penned, and a wagon is kept.

The road is deep
And in some places steep,
Highbanked, and hollowed by man and horse
Whose footsteps still creep
Through a ghostly sleep
Of Celts, and Romans, and Saxons, and Norse.

Nomads first made
This highway for trade
While they roamed in search of new grass to graze;
Their herds were a spade
Through heather and glade
In years that are hidden behind a haze.

Eternity's eye
Saw Time passing by;
Stone Age, and Bronze Age, and Iron Age, and then
—While the flint-sparks fly
To an ancient sky—
The first hybrid legion of Englishmen.

BEREAVED

You think it inconceivable,
Yet I believe it possible,
That—when the months have cauterised
This wound which holds you agonised—
You will once more participate
In things which now seem out-of-date.
The April birds shall serenade,
And you will hear them undismayed;
True friendship's loving regiment
Shall share your dark predicament;
Laughter, which now seems blasphemy,

Shall prove good humour's alchemy;
And you will rhyme " activity "
To reason with " futility ".
This is not kind encouragement;
It is life's harsh arbitrement
Whereby the soul's Gethsemane
May sometimes show itself to be
A phoenix that with wounded wing
Arose above its suffering.

ENGLAND

Spirit of England, living
Among the hills and dales,
Ever to good men giving
A breeze that swells the sails:

Still through the fashions' houring
You shine at heart the same,
A rose revived and flowering
Under an ancient name.

Still with the dawn a farmer
Interrogates the sky,
Wishing the weather calmer,
Cursing a brook run dry.

Still the old gossips mutter
Passing a time of day
Ever anon to utter
Some scandalous hearsay.

Still among country places
A manor house maintains
The grandeur and the graces
Of its ancestral reigns.

Still from the inn's seclusion
The cottagers debate
Scarcity and profusion
And themes of high estate.

Still from a village steeple
The pealing bells declare:
"Come all to church, good people,
And praise the Lord in prayer."

Still from our English beaches
Over a worldwide haul
The bold White Ensign reaches
Her lawful ports-of-call.

Still at their market-tether
The cows and sheep complain
While honey haunts the heather
And fields unfold the grain.

Still through a summer gloaming
The lovers steal away
Down by the river roaming
To prattle and to play.

Still when the light has faded,
Old men beside a stile
Recall when they paraded
Mile upon marching mile.

So from a steadfast quorum
The folk of England give
In saecula saeculorum
The love by which they live.

ON HEARING THE FIRST CUCKOO IN SPRING

Two notes alone,
So narrowing
Yet of a tone
So harrowing
That, from their fallow music, flies
A phoenix, with an old surprise
Deep-marrowing
The essence of a bone which never dies.

What poet can
So well deploy
From such small span
So great a joy?
No voice nor melic instrument
Survey so vast a firmament;
No skills employ
An artifice so stripped of ornament.

The song is bare;
Its message plain;
The twofold air
Recites again
What no man ever tired to hear
... A welcome for a fledgling year
Whose sun and rain
Play hide-and-seek, then fade, then reappear.

So, out of two
Are many viewed,
And from that brew
A multitude
Distilled, while past and future seem
To wake within a jumbled dream
Once more imbued
With out-of-date realities come true.

TONIGHT

How many hearts that mourn tonight,
Or fear, or hate, or beat
Alone in unregarded blight
That circulates defeat?

What is the total sum of pain
In body and in mind,
The worldwide rub against the grain
Of suffering mankind?

Mankind itself lacks wit to know
Its own immense distress;
There are no registers that show
The whole unhappiness:

And if there were, no man could learn
The answer, and be sane;
Horror beyond belief would burn
The tissues of his brain.

GREENSLEEVES

It was at such a time as this,
All on a Mayday morning,
That he whose name we do not know
Strolled through a meadow white as snow
Where blossom bleached the ground as though
Manna had fallen there to show
The site of sorrow's overthrow.

The sun stood high, a cuckoo called,
Echo on echo rising
While he the nameless English man
Walked where a tireless river ran
Under a glinting green-bough span
Of lucent beech-leaves like a fan
In Eden when the world began.

The age of pain withdrew awhile,
Purged by an hour of gladness,
And silently he scored the sound
Of deep thanksgiving gladly bound
To acres of a homely ground
Where every faithful seeker found
Contentment by enchantment crowned.

Four hundred years and more have passed
Since first he sang his Matins
To heal the autumn's sombre smart
And winter's penetrating dart;
A song so plain that every heart
Hearing the unobtrusive art
Has ever after hummed its part.

O lovely land, O happy time,
O music well-remembered!
Be to us still as once of old
When all the world was young and bold,
And from the valley and the wold
A multitude of birds foretold
Moments of magic manifold.

MIDSUMMER NIGHT

Dies the day dim
Watching a moon
Raising her rim
On night's lagoon.
Over the hills
Faint in the west
Daylight distils
Blood from its breast,
And the dumb vale
Darkens to be
Speckled with pale
Star galaxy.
Counting the hours
Slower than men,
Two village towers
Multiply ten,
And the hay lies
Pillowed in scent
While a bat flies
Where the bee went.

. . . ET FINEM PERFECTAM

Few men achieve that perfect end
Which I have seen a bird obtain
When, seeming merely to descend,
It soared beyond the reach of pain.

So would I go, in harness still,
Before the hand can clutch the heart,
Before the dread can daunt the will,
Before the eye can see the dart:

Or, best of all, without a dream
To fall asleep, and not to know
That I have crossed the lethal stream
... Unless I wake, and find it so.

EDWARD THOMAS: KILLED IN ACTION 1917

The gods half-loved you, for your death occurred
Upon the brink of middle age, before
The rodent winds of wintertime were heard
Gnawing at autumn's unprotected door.
You died before your fame was born, and so
You did not live to mourn its own decay,
Nor watch the tidal fashion ebb-and-flow,
Sweeping tomorrow back to yesterday.
Your kestrel-eye was never dimmed; your hair
Not plucked nor frosted; to the end you strode
Four miles an hour, too fast for you to share
Methuselah's unenviable load.
Old age would not have suited you at all;
The dice were kind that threw your early fall.

MAKE-AND-MEND

Hark, my heart, the waves are calling,
Happy on the morning air;
See the foam-flake fairy-falling
And the white gulls everywhere.

Breathe, my soul, the brine of breakers
Surging through the flaccid blood
Like a dove that dares the acres
Of a universal Flood.

Watch the playful wavelets sidling
Softly on a summer sand;
Reap the depths of leisure, idling
Far away from Mammonland.

Hear again your old ship ploughing
Sibilantly through the sea,
To a westward bounty bowing
With intrepid courtesy.

Though an inland ill attend you,
And the sands of Time assault,
Still the sea shall make-and-mend you
Gay as sunlight, firm as gault.

NEW YEAR'S EVE

A cold night,
A clear moon,
The stars bright
And thick-strewn.

Firelight flows
From the door
Like a rose
On the floor.

The sheep graze,
The fell bides,
The church prays,
The beck glides.

From the spheres
Swinging round
Silence hears
Not a sound.

This is bare
Beauty, caught
On an air
Keenly wrought.

MOONSTRUCK

Mankind has walked upon the Moon,
And nevermore shall we perceive
The majesty of night's high noon
Without our deeper senses grieve
To think that something of the ancient light
Has passed beyond, because within, our sight.

Mankind has set its mark upon
The mystic features of a myth
Which in imagination shone
New-minted by a silversmith
In phases; but that iridescent Queen
Now bares her secret self behind the scene.

O Lady, you have lost at last
The gracious style of chivalry;
The years of your mystique are past
And all the poets' fantasy.
No more a Sovereign Lady of the Night,
You must submit to be a satellite.

LIGHT AND SHADE

The storm has passed,
And now at last
What music from the bushes
Where curlews cry
While blackbirds vie
With thrushes.

One-half the world
Is pastel-pearled
With mournful greyness quailing
Before the bright
Triumphant light
Prevailing.

The flowers look up
To quiz a cup
Of sunshine after shadows,
And all the hills
Are watermills
For meadows.

Where else to see
So vividly
The moods of man's subsistence?
From light and shade
The gods have made
Existence.

LULLABY

Soliciting sleep, with my face to the hills,
I picture the moonbeam that silverly spills
On stags while they lie in a heatherbed combe
Where rivulets run like a murmurous loom.

I picture the wood, and a path through the brake
Where moonlight and midnight have mated to make
Euphonious silence, and etched it to seem
The sharp silhouette of a black-and-white dream.

I picture the ponies that graze on the moor,
And glow-worms like milestones along a dim spoor.
I picture the sea at the foot of those heights,
Encompassed by cliffs that are steep stalagmites.

I picture the lanes that delve deeper than moles
Through primrosing banks and the beeches' grey boles;
I picture the farmhouse whose cob walls are white
As mushrooms that sprang from the soil overnight.

All aspects and features fall neatly in place
While the visionless hills peer down on my face;
And each, as I count them, becomes like a sheep
Which enters the turnstile that lulls me asleep.

TIME

We call it Time, although we do not know
Time's nature; at the best, we may observe
Time's aftermath, and trace the swift or slow
Parabola of seismographic curve.
When least we crave it, we have most to spare;
When most we seek it, little then remains;
The brimful larder stealthily grows bare
Of every thing except the crumbs and stains.
When least we fear to lose it, Time stands still;
When most we fear to feel it, Time then flies,
And age becomes at last a codicil
Bequeathed by childhood as a grim surprise
Calculated to take away our breath
When Time forsakes us on the brink of death.

TRANSITORY

Find comfort when you can;
It will not wait on you.
Where summer rivers ran
Winter may thirst for dew.
Feel thankful if the rain
Sometimes returns again
To slake the withered grass
Of streams that came, to pass.

Take comfort by the hand;
It will not lead you on
Toward a wonderland
That was, and now is gone.
Feel thankful if you see
Glimpses of Arcady
Like flowers at Candlemas
That bloomed awhile, to pass.

Treat comfort with reserve;
It has no need of you;
A multitude deserve
The fortune of the few.
Feel thankful if it stay
But for another day,
Since comfort ever was
A thing that came, to pass.

PREDICTION

I have seen fashions rise and fall like nations
That deemed themselves immortal, yet were laid
Low in the sand by drastic innovations
Whose burial was unburied by a spade.

So, I predict, old courtesy shall find
New lodgings at an inn as yet unborn;
A decorous love of lineage shall bind
Strangers in sheaves amid their native corn.

Duty once more shall pay its own reward;
Eros shall wear discarded modesty;
The servant shall not rank before his lord,
Nor freedom pave a path for anarchy.

Faith shall be fathered in despair's despite;
True joy shall shame false wit's compulsive jeers;
And sonnets shall be sung again, to light
A second dark-eyed woman down the years.

BRETHREN

If men from time to time
Strode naked through the street
Their modesty might climb
Above its own defeat.

Such likeness to a beast
Would brand them one and all,
The greatest and the least
Being an animal.

For pity's sake alone
Humanity would be
Accustomed to condone
Its consanguinity.

ARMCHAIR TRAVELLER

How many battles I have won,
How many castles I have spun,
How many favours I have done
While dreaming by the fire.

How many pledges I have made,
How many Odysseys essayed,
How many journeyings delayed
While dreaming by the fire.

How many epics I have planned,
How many rivers I have spanned,
How many habits I have banned
While dreaming by the fire.

How many guises I have worn,
How many veiling curtains torn,
How many crucifixions borne
While dreaming by the fire.

There, in the leaping light, I see
The warmer years that used to be,
And winter closing-in on me
While dreaming by the fire.

WINTER FUEL

Their lifespan now fulfilled,
These leaves have overspilled
To make a mild yet mellow
Compost of red and yellow
That spreads its wintry fruits
Above the hidden roots.

In circles they are laid
As by a magic spade
That sprinkles them concisely,
Evenly, and precisely
Where the long roots most need
Their self-assembled feed:

And over them, just so,
The dripping branches grow
To slake the yeasty solid
With mineral-tinted liquid:
So simple, so adroit,
This annual exploit

BEETHOVEN

Greatest and best belov'd of all whose art
Has voyaged upon strange seas of thought, alone;
Who saw, but could not hear, the world depart,
Leaving him to the echoes of his own
Soundless companionship, from whose dumb height
Art spoke to him and sang to him. Buffoon,
Braggart, and naïve worlding each in turn;
The puppet of affection's fickle tune,
Aching for love, yet destined still to yearn;
Within that comic-tragedy of loss,
That deaf, unkempt, pathetic isolation
. . . There burned the lamp which cauterised the dross,
And lit the dungeon of its desolation.
His music scaled the euphony of Time;
Manly, and gay, and tender, and sublime.

VERNAL

Consult the records, and you find
That men have hungered for the spring
Since Bartimaeus, being blind,
Rejoiced to hear the blackbird sing
Merrily to his mate
That sat in high estate
Nursing her nestlings while a breeze
Rocked the slow cradle of the trees.

The long Dark Ages kept one light
To cheer them on their woeful way,
Kindled when hedgerows wear a white
Whimple to welcome Easter Day.
The rugged Saxon rhymes
Hailed those redeeming times,
As Noah from his anxious Ark
Hailed the lone dove, life's dauntless spark.

In England's greenly pleasant land,
Where Chaucer rode to Becket's shrine,
The poets felt their fervour fanned
When April blended shower and shine;
Aloud with one accord
They offered to the Lord
New songs upon an ancient theme,
The death of winter's dismal scheme.

When Philip sent his ships from Spain
With bell and book and candle, sworn
To sweep the English from the main,
And kill them in their native corn,
Still with a varied voice
The poets sang their choice
... April and May and early June,
The months of colour, scent, and tune.

While England warred within a realm
Of Roundheads and of Cavaliers,
One poet seized the lyric helm,
Foremost among his singing peers;

Herrick, whose mastered art
Revealed a vernal heart
In love with spring's too-mortal hours
Of rising grass and fading flowers.

In later years the mountains bred
A boy who roamed from crag to crag,
Keen as an eagle's eye that led
Toward the lurking moorland stag;
Wordsworth, the grown boy
For whom the spring spelt joy
Writ large above the sombre reign
Of life's interminable pain.

So, down the ages, spring has been
A gentle Consort of the Year,
Chosen by all to rule as Queen
Till summer heralds reappear;
And still her own writ runs
Among her singing sons,
Her poets, who with husky voice
Echo their fathers' melic choice.

Welcome, dear season; thaw our blood
So long so cold with winter's dearth.
Open your sluices warmly; flood
Blossom and birdsong through the Earth;
Summon the sun to rise
As monarch of the skies.
Let lambs abound, and bluebells ring;
Lift up our hearts, that we may sing.

CAVEAT

Do not abide in solitude
Unless you would become
Alone with that beatitude
Whose parts exceed your sum.

God is the sole companion
Of solitary men;
He, only, their communion,
A Crescent, Cross, or Zen.

Without that rapt addition
The lonely pilgrim goes
Naked through Time's attrition
And Thought's corrosive snows.

His single grief is legion;
His finite fear, unbound;
His joy, a barren region;
His hope, a hollow sound.

A FROSTY MORNING

Like slender penguins now
The burdened branches bow
While hoarbells tinkle as they freeze,
And snowflakes curtsy on a breeze
To grace the ground below.

With more than ploughman's art
An early-morning cart
Indents its mark along the lane
Where robins think the grit is grain
That will not peck apart.

Each holly bush is spiced
With sugar never iced
By human hand; and one old oak
Lies stricken by a sharper stroke
... The frost, that left it spliced.

Within the wood no stir
Except a wanderer
Crunching his homeward way; no bird
Is visible, no squirrel heard;
No feather and no fur.

The whitened wizardry
Creates a fantasy
So eloquent it stabs the sight
With inarticulate delight
At winter's artistry.

TO HIS SHIP

Wind, blow;
Let-go
The hawser of my spirit,
That she may show her merit
Long-learned from ancient storms on seas
Where ships are battered to their knees
Yet whitely re-arise
With bowsprite to the skies.

Blow, wind;
Unbind
The stay-sheets and the shackle
And all a seaman's tackle
. . . The rein and bit with which he rides
A scudding ship that deftly glides
Upward and down undaunted
Though tempested and taunted.

O wind,
In mind
I feel again the shudder
Of waves around the rudder
In my old ship; again I feel
My hand upon her spinning wheel,
And in my heart for aye
The sting of healing spray.

Wind, slip
My ship,
My lovely one, a kiss
In memory of bliss.
She was my child, my mother,
My mistress; to each other
Through fair and foul we pledged a vow,
And kept it all her lifetime. Now
She rests where she would be,
Buried beneath the sea.

FIRE

Co-aeval with a caveman
Encompassed by the night,
This fire of sticks engenders
Precautionary warmth.

Countless the nightly beacons
That down the years have blazed
Since flint and twig delivered
Prometheus from harm.

Crouching beside this bonfire,
I am the same as they
Who heard the wolves, and clustered
Gregarious as sheep.

Perennial the instinct
To promulgate a fire
While darkness and the winter
Remain uncivilised.

HYMN TO THE SUN

To thee ascends my soul,
O Sun, that first and last
Invites us to extol
The beauty of a vast
Horizon crowned by beeches
Whose royal-topgallant reaches
With ever-open palms
To supplicate for alms.

To thee the bluebells ring
Matins and Evensong
Which consecrate the spring,
And right the winter's wrong
With carillons whose colour
Obliterates all dolour,
Spreading a silent shroud
That paints the land aloud.

To thee the young lambs bleat,
And frisk their sooty tails;
Thou art the living heat
By which the corn prevails.
Blind though they are, the windows
Wink to behold thee; shadows
Scatter a pitch-black light
Over their noonday night.

To thee the rivers rise
And shine like silver fish;
The waves invoke thine eyes;
The wells fulfil thy wish.
Oceans at thy reveille
Dance an obeisant ballet;
All waters everywhere
Return thy smiling stare.

To thee the birds awake
With calls that echo through
The sleeping woods, and make
Old melodies anew.
At rising and at setting
Thou art their song's begetting;
Thy sinking in the west
Is their nocturnal nest.

Even the snows—that fade
To feel thy warm approach—
Even the snows are made
A little while to broach
Blue summer's brilliant prospect,
And with their own white aspect
To dazzle till they blind
Beauty's astonished mind.

To thee our fathers knelt,
And raised prodigious stones
With symmetry that spelt
The gratitude of bones
Released from winter's rigour
By thine ascendant vigour:
We also are beholden,
The progeny of Eden.

HYMNS ANCIENT AND MODERN

" A dole of bread, a crock of wine,
A spear to keep your guard unfurled:
Beloved, with these gifts of mine
Go forth against the other world."

" A wreath of flowers, a sculptured grave,
Remembered for a little time:
Beloved, what is left to save
Out of the years' erosive rime?"

On ignorance we build a faith
That was ten thousand years ago:
New knowledge cannot parse the wraith,
Nor tell us why it needs be so.

FREEHOLD

I call it mine,
And on the line
I duly sign
My name; yet these few fields and this one house
Apparently belong to any mouse
That makes its bed
In my wood-shed.

The birds that sit
Or fly and flit
For the tit-bit
I throw to them; the tall red stags; the sheep
Penned in a paddock; and the owls which keep
Late hours . . . each swears
That mine is theirs.

Raucous and slow,
Rooks come and go
All day as though
They held the freehold. Fishes in the pool,
Badgers and flowers and bees and that toadstool
. . . All seem to claim
The owner's name.

And what are these
Dumb fantasies
Among the trees?
They are the folk—three centuries of ghosts—
Who in their season likewise played the hosts

To every guest
Except the pest.

Aloud or dumb,
Let them all come
To swell the sum
Of those who lived here and of those unborn
Who, when I die, shall mow my garden lawn
While Time re-reads
The title deeds.

NOBLESSE OBLIGE

Of your charity, pray for them
With whom no others kneel
—The unremembered ones, that were
Forgotten by the fold.

Of your plenitude, bid them come,
Nor wait for them, but go
Into the byeways shepherdlike
With cordial crozier.

Of your happiness, let them broach
A cask that is not theirs,
To share with you the ageless wine
Of universal love.

Of your courtesy, condescend
To bow to their duresse;
So shall your meek obeisance raze
Their unprotected pride.

FILL-DYKE

Mud, mud is February's blood,
And it seeps from every vein
Like the sludging silt of a fill-dyke flood
That follows the wake of rain.

Soft, soft sighs the mountain path
That summer once scorched to steel,
For a toecap slides on the aftermath
Of the shepherd's cautious heel.

Deep, deep delves the byre-bilge now,
Cliffed to a tall man's calf;
And the wagon wheel is a churning plough,
And the fetlock hid by half.

Slop, slop say the beechwood leaves
With never a crisp reply
From the farmer's stick that damply weaves
A way toward the sty.

All, all is Sargasso soft
Within the house and out,
From the kitchen mat to the apple loft;
And shall be, till a drought.

A DAY TO REMEMBER

I walked the meadows early
While April turned to May,
And all the lambs were curly,
And all the grass was gay.

Woods on the wind were waving;
Daffodils danced to be;
Larks were an incense, paving
Heaven with harmony.

Never (the blackbird chanted)
Had joy adown the years
With such insistence granted
A benefice of tears;

Tears of an ancient wonder,
Bright as a jewel that crept
From sorrow's rusty plunder,
Too happy to be wept.

WISHING WELL

Peace to your heart this Easter Day,
And joy and all endeavour;
About this hour you kneel to pray,
Believing in a Saviour.

Of all who in my heyday crossed
The path that led before me,
You were the one most loved, most lost;
The saviour to restore me.

A wanderer, I found you fixed;
Faithful, you found me creedless;
Had those extremes by me been mixed,
This elegy were needless.

You are in woman's summer now,
And I draw near to winter;
The mistletoe upon the bough
Impaled me with a splinter.

And yet indeed I wish you well,
Fulfilling so my duty,
For on me once you wove a spell
Of gentleness and beauty.

CHRISTMAS FARE

Arising with the dawn,
A robin pecks the lawn,
Then hops beside the door
As though to ask for more.
He shall not seek in vain from this
My hilltop house and his hospice.

Does he not sing while some
Are seasonally dumb?
Does he not bide at home
While swifts and swallows roam
Through distant lands? He is indeed
A Briton of the ancient breed.

Come, robin, to the feast;
On Christmas Day at least,
All doors are open, each
Within the memory's reach
Though far away, or gone at last
Into the archives of the past.

IDES OF MARCH

Rooks cawing, and the evening
Star like a dewdrop leavening
The dusky spectrum of a dying day:
Bare beeches suckling silently
The copper buds that patiently
Abide till April flings their sheath away.

Lambs bleating, and the benefice
Of barley's rising edifice,
And fresh-turned furrows for an autumn yield:
A solo thrush sings Evensong
While murmurously all day long
The brook meanders through a kingcup field.

From far away the clamorous
Bark of a fox whose amorous
Echoes are answered by censorious owls:
Imbued with frail resilience,
Daffodils droop like penitents
Rapt in the cloister of their yellow cowls.

Winter, about to abdicate,
Raises himself to contemplate
The heir whom he is powerless to disown:
Spring, modest in her tutelage,
Restrains the surging equipage
Wherewith she comes to claim a toppling throne.

THE LAND

The land is lonely now;
A tractor-man can plough
More furrows in one hour
Than any horse-hauled power.
He rides alone, where formerly there walked
Three jingling teams abreast, that sang and talked.

The haytime is a swift
And reeking roar; no drift
Of badinage while scythes
Sweep swathes through hills and hythes.
The task of twenty mowers now employs
Two witless tractors and two wordless boys.

Over a stubbled loam
The harvest hurries home
To television; all
The coloured carnival
Has gone, and all the gratitude that led
To man's thanksgiving for his daily bread.

Now the land is lonely,
Reaped and tilled by only
A remnant of the folk
Who bore its heavy yoke,
Beneath whose weight they often rose, with health
And cheerfulness of heart, their richest wealth.

CORNISH CREAM

Columb, Clether, Clement, Issey,
Breock, Breward, Veep, and Just;
Mewgan, Mawgan, Minven, Levan,
Ive, Portscatho, Roseland, Erth;
Baragwanath, Trink, Lamorna,
Plain-an-Gwarry, Come-To-Good,
Sancreed, Trencrum, Indian Queens,
Praze-an-Beeble, Zone, Chykembro,
Wheals of Damsel, Rose, and Jewel;
Mawla, Morvah, Marazion,
Amalabrea, Chyandor.

AUTOBIOGRAPHY

Content you with my songs,
And leave the rest to chance;
All other rights or wrongs
Being irrelevance.

The furrows fiercely limed
By blizzard and by heat
Were merely rungs that climbed
Toward a winnowed wheat.

Content you with that wheat,
And let the ploughman die,
For in his songs you meet
The essence that was I.

CONCLUSION

Now unto God commend we all our souls,
To whom imagination may not soar,
Nor reason force a barred and bolted door,
Nor comprehension plumb uncharted shoals.
If he exist, then to his grace we go
Penitent in our gracelessness, and loud
With intercession for the hearts we know
And on earth love. By many bruises bowed,
We bleed; yet still, amid that poignant flow,
Beauty abides, and laughter, and a deep
Remembrance of the men who here below
Sowed heavenly comfort for the world to **reap.**
Now unto God our unbelief ascends,
That he himself may make his own amends.